D0426875

Getting Started in Science

Experiments with
Bubbles

Robert Gardner

E N S L O W   P U B L I S H E R S ,   I N C .

44 Fadem Road   P.O. Box 38
Box 699   Aldershot
Springfield, N.J. 07081   Hants GU12 6BP
U.S.A.   U.K.

Library of Congress Cataloging-in-Publication Data

Gardner, Robert, 1929–
    Experiments with bubbles / Robert Gardner.
        p. cm. — (Getting started in science)
    Includes bibliographical references and index.
    Summary: A collection of experiments that use bubbles to illustrate scientific
principles and properties.
    ISBN 0-89490-666-6
    1. Bubbles—Experiments—Juvenile literature. [1. Bubbles—Experiments. 2.
Experiments.] I. Title. II. Series: Gardner, Robert, 1929–Getting started in science.
QC183.G26 1995
530.4′275′078—dc20

                                                    95–14619
                                                      CIP
                                                      AC

Printed in the United States of America

10 9 8 7 6 5 4 3

Illustration Credits: Kimberly Austin Daly

Cover Illustration: Enslow Publishers, Inc.

Contents

Introduction 4

1 Bubbles and More Bubbles 7

2 Bubble Chemistry 17

3 The Life and Size of Bubbles 39

4 Bubbles in Motion 56

5 Bubbles, Light, and Color 73

6 Bubble Geometry 85

Answers to Puzzlers
and Surprises 95

Further Reading 101

Index 102

Introduction

Blowing bubbles is not only fun, it is also a good way to get started in science. Bubbles provide an enjoyable pathway to science because they can serve as the basis for many experiments—experiments that involve light, color, chemistry, force, air pressure, electricity, buoyancy, floating, density, and other science-related ideas and activities.

Experiments with Bubbles will allow you to carry out experiments using simple everyday objects and materials more often associated with play than with science. These experiments will lead you to a number of scientific discoveries, principles, and measuring techniques. They will help you to learn how science works, because you will be investigating the world as scientists do.

Some experiments will be preceded or followed by an explanation of a scientific principle. In some cases, the explanation will involve doing additional experiments in order to help you better understand the principle. Once you understand the basic idea, you should have enough information to allow you to answer questions and interpret results in the experiments related to the principle. Some of these experiments might start you on a path leading to a science fair project.

A few puzzlers and surprises related to the experiments are scattered throughout the book. The answers to some of these puzzlers and surprises can be found by doing more experiments. The answers to others are located at the back of the book. But don't turn to the answers right away. See if you can come up with your own solutions to the problems and questions first. Then compare your answers with the ones given.

The experiments and activities included in this book were chosen because they can be investigated with bubbles. Most of them are safe and can be done without expensive equipment. If an experiment requires the use of a knife, a flame, or anything that has a potential for danger, you will be asked to work with an adult. Please do so! The purpose of such a request is to protect you from getting hurt.

To make bubbles, you will need a bubble-making solution that contains soap. You can buy ready-made solutions in bottles that come with bubble wands. However, you can make your own bubble solutions with dishwashing liquid and water. In a number of experiments, you will be asked to prepare and test different bubble-making solutions. When you make your own solutions, it is important that you use rainwater or bottled water that you can buy at a grocery store. Hard water (water that contains minerals) reacts with soap and makes it more difficult to blow bubbles.

A bubble's skin, which seems to us so thin, is really hundreds of molecules thick.

Bubbles and More Bubbles

In this chapter you will discover some of the many ways you can make bubbles. Take time to enjoy the beautiful but fragile bubbles as they drift in the air. Watch them fall. Watch them move in the wind—sometimes upward, sometimes downward, sometimes sideways. Look at the brightly colored images that are reflected from both the front and back of each bubble. Notice that the images reflected in the bubbles have different colors than the objects themselves.

Later, you will have a chance to explore the science found in bubbles, but for now, just have fun making and watching them.

1.1 MAKING BUBBLES

To do this experiment you will need:

- materials to make bubble wands and pipes: plastic drinking straw, tin can with top and bottom removed, paper cup, Styrofoam cup, paper sheet, mason jar lid, funnel, baster, eyedropper, plastic or rubber tubing, screening, plastic berry basket, pipe cleaner, rubber or metal washer, rubber band, string, wire, or any other items you think might serve for making bubbles
- bubble-making solution (you can make your own by dissolving one cup of liquid dishwashing detergent in two cups of soft water. Stir gently to avoid suds.)
- old newspapers
- glasses or safety goggles (optional)

You are going to make lots and lots of bubbles. But bubbles are made from soap films and soap is slippery and messy. If it is a warm, calm day, you may want to blow bubbles outdoors. Be sure you do not let the bubbles or the solution fall on steps or walks. It could make them slippery and dangerous.

Soap Bubbles

If you are going to be inside, spread newspapers over the area where you plan to make bubbles. Keep the bubble-making solution in a wide container. If you buy the bubble-making solution and try to keep it in the bottle it came in, it is very likely that you will spill it. Sometimes a bursting bubble will spatter some soap onto your face. If you do not like the stinging that happens when you get soap in your eye, wear glasses or safety goggles.

You have probably made bubbles using a bottle of bubble-making solution. You dip one end of the plastic wand that comes with the solution into the bottle and wave it through the air to produce a bevy of bubbles, as shown in Figure 1. You may also have found that you can make bubbles by dipping the wand into the

1) Making bubbles with a wand and bubble-making solution.

solution and blowing gently against the film that forms across the open portion of the wand. Can you use your thumb and fingers to make a wand and blow bubbles from your hands?

Bubble Wands

Was there something about a bubble wand that required careful research by an inventor? Or can almost anything be used to make bubbles? To find out, make bubbles using as many of the objects listed above as you can find. Try things of your own design that are not listed. Which of the things that you tried can be used as bubble wands? What is the common characteristic of all the wands that work? Which ones cannot be used as bubble wands?

Can a wand with a square opening be used to make bubbles? Do the bubbles produced with such a wand have a square (cubic) shape? Can a wand with an odd-shaped opening be used to make bubbles? If so, what are the shape of the bubbles?

What seems to determine whether you get a big bubble or a small one? If you blow bubbles using a can or a cup, does the length of the can or cup make any difference? Does the diameter of the wand make a difference?

1.2   A BUBBLE PIPE

To do this experiment you will need:
- bubble-making solution
- plastic drinking straw
- small (5- or 6-ounce) Styrofoam cup
- pencil
- small paper cup
- wide, shallow container to hold solution

Bubble-making solutions used to come with bubble pipes instead of wands. The bowl of the pipe was turned over and dipped into the soapy liquid. Then air was blown gently into the stem of the pipe to make a bubble on the bowl.

You can make your own bubble pipe. Use a pencil to make a hole near the bottom of a small Styrofoam cup, as shown in Figure 2. Then push a plastic drinking straw through the hole and into the cup. Turn the cup upside down and dip it into the bubble-making solution. When you remove the cup, you should be able to see

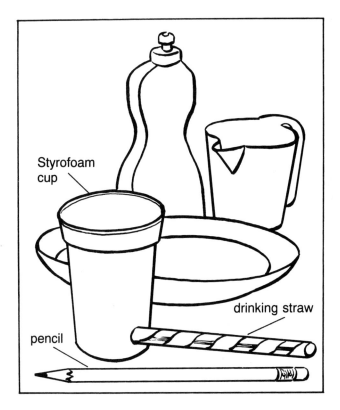

Styrofoam cup

drinking straw

pencil

2) You can make your own bubble pipe.

11

a soap film stretched across the cup. Blow gently into the straw to form a bubble on the top of the cup.

With a little practice, you will find that you can twist the cup and set the bubble free. Can you catch the bubble on the cup? What happens if you try to catch the bubble on a cup that has not been dipped in the bubble-making solution? Can you catch a bubble if your hand is dry? Can you catch a bubble if your hand is wet with water? Can you catch a bubble if your hand is wet with soapy water?

Can you use a paper cup to make a bubble pipe? Does it work as well as the Styrofoam cup? What else can you use to make a bubble pipe?

Catch a bubble on your bubble pipe. Look at the images you see in the soap film. Light reflected from the bubble surfaces forms the images you see. Can you see images on the front surface of the bubble? Can you see images on the rear surface? Which images are upside down? What happens to the color seen in these images as the soap film drains and evaporates?

1.3   BIG BUBBLES

To do this experiment you will need:
- bubble-making solution
- heavy string and fuzzy yarn
- shallow container longer than a drinking straw
- scissors
- plastic drinking straws

Making giant bubbles is a lot of fun, but you need a wide open space to make them. Find a place outdoors on a day when there is very little wind. Place a long, shallow container on a level area. Pour enough bubble-making solution into the pan to cover it to a depth of about 2–3 centimeters (1 inch).

A Giant Bubble Wand

Use scissors to cut off about 1 meter (3 feet) of heavy string. Run the string through two drinking straws and tie a knot. This will form a rectangular wand, as shown in

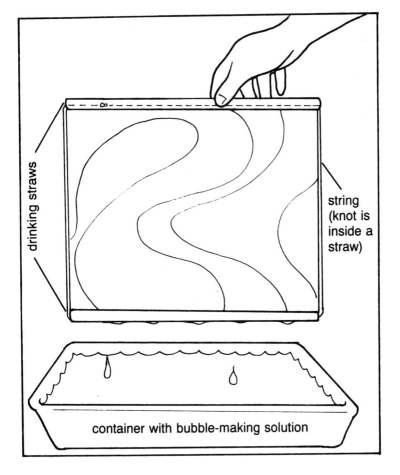

drinking straws

string (knot is inside a straw)

container with bubble-making solution

3) A wand for making giant bubbles.

Figure 3. Place the wand (both straws and string), and your thumbs and fingers in the bubble solution. Bring the straws together and be sure that the string is totally submerged. Then lift the wand slowly from the container. Move the straws apart. You should see a soap film stretched across the rectangular wand. Pull the extended wand upward through the air, stretching the film into a cylindrical bubble. (A cylinder has the shape of a soup can; a sphere has the shape of a ball or the earth.) Then bring the straws together to close off the soap film and form a giant bubble. Is the bubble you have made a cylinder or a sphere?

Launching Giant Bubbles

If you do not succeed at first, keep trying. You will find that with practice you can form very large bubbles. Notice how they move as they travel through the air. Look at the many colors reflected from the soap film.

Occasionally, you will find that a film remains on the wand after you have launched a giant bubble. This film is thinner than the one you started with because much of that first film is in the bubble you made. Make a second bubble with this thinner film. Because the soap film is so thin, it weighs less than the first bubble. Therefore, it is more likely to float up into the air.

Make another giant bubble wand using fuzzy yarn instead of string. Which wand seems to make better bubbles, the one made of yarn or the one made of string?

See if you can make a wand that will allow you to make even bigger bubbles.

1.4 BREAKING AND NON-BREAKING BUBBLES

To do this experiment you will need:
- Bubble-making solution and wand
- woolen blanket
- shallow container

You know that bubbles often break when they touch something, but sometimes they do not. To find out why bubbles break, pour some bubble-making solution into a shallow container, dip a wand into the solution and blow some bubbles. What happens when you touch a bubble with a dry finger? What happens to a bubble that lands on a dry surface? What happens to a bubble that falls on your arm?

Wet your finger with some of the bubble-making solution. Does the bubble break when you touch it with your wet finger? Rub some of the liquid on your arm. Do bubbles break when they land on your soapy arm?

Let some bubbles fall onto a dry woolen blanket. Why don't the bubbles break when they land on the blanket? Can you make other bubbles bounce off the bubbles that are on the blanket? Can you make apple-size bubbles bounce off the blanket?

PUZZLER 1.1
Why do bubbles break when they touch your dry finger, but not when they touch your wet finger? Why don't bubbles break when they fall on a woolen blanket? Compare you answer to the one on page 95.

1.5   WATER BUBBLES

To do this experiment you will need:

- wide, shallow container
- plastic drinking straw
- water
- dishwashing liquid

You have blown bubbles on a wand and on a pipe, and you have made bubbles by swinging a wand to fill the soap film stretched across the wand with air. Now see what you can do about making bubbles with just plain water.

Find a wide, clean, shallow container. Rinse it thoroughly with water to wash away any soap that might be in it. Add some water to the container. Then, using a drinking straw, blow bubbles in the water. Do bubbles form? What happens to the water bubbles after they rise to the surface?

Next, add two or three drops of dishwashing liquid to the water. Mix the soap into the water gently with the straw. Can you blow bubbles in the water now using the straw? Do they last longer than the water bubbles?

What a difference a drop or two of soap can make! In the next chapter, you will try to find out why water bubbles collapse, but soapy water bubbles persist.

As water evaporates from a bubble's surface, its "skin" becomes thinner. Because gravity pulls liquids downward, the bottom side of a bubble or soap film is thicker than the top.

Bubble Chemistry

Normally, when someone says something is sticky, you think of syrup, honey, or molasses. If your fingers are covered with honey, they stick together and to everything you touch. To get them clean, you wash them with soap and water. But chemists will tell you that water is "sticky" too. It's not sticky in the same way as honey, but it does stick to itself. In this chapter, you will investigate water's "stickiness." By carrying out experiments, you will see that water holds together very well indeed. In fact, it is so sticky that its bubbles collapse as you saw in Chapter 1. Adding soap to water makes it less sticky. A soap solution sticks together with just the right force to surround air and form what we call bubbles—bubbles that do not collapse the way water bubbles do.

2.1   STICKY WATER IN A CUP

To do this experiment you will need:
- water
- table fork
- medicine cup, plastic vial, or small plastic cup
- eyedropper
- paper clip or needle
- plastic container

Fill a clean medicine cup, plastic vial, or small plastic cup with water. Fill it right up to the brim, so that the water is even with the top of the cup or vial. Then use an eyedropper to see how many drops of water you can add to an already full container. You will be amazed by how high you can pile water above the rim. How many drops above "full" did you add? What would happen in this experiment if water did not stick together?

4) Use a table fork to place a paper clip or a needle on the surface of some water.

Leave the water heaped above the rim of the cup or vial. You can return to it in Experiment 2.2. Meanwhile, use a table fork to place a steel paper clip or needle on the surface of some water in another plastic container (see Figure 4). If you are careful in placing the steel object on the water, you will find that it will float on the water's surface. It is as if the water has a skin. You can even see where the skin bends to support the steel object. It looks much like your own skin when you push on it with your finger.

2.2   MAKING WATER LESS STICKY

To do this experiment you will need:
- water
- bar of soap
- medicine cup, plastic vial, or small plastic cup
- eyedropper
- faucet
- penny

Return to the water-filled cup or vial you prepared in Experiment 2.1. To that water heaped above the rim of the vessel, add just one drop of soapy water. What happens? How does soap affect water's stickiness?

What do you think will happen if you add a drop of soapy water to the container in which a paper clip or needle is floating? Try it! Were you right? What effect does soap have on water's skin?

How many drops of water can you place on a penny? Be sure to use a clean eyedropper that has been rinsed well to remove any soap. Once you have heaped as many drops as possible on the penny, predict what will happen if you touch the water with the corner of a bar of soap. Were you right?

At the end of a leaky faucet, water heaps in an up-side-down fashion to form drops that fall into the sink. Turn on a faucet until drops of water fall from it at a slow rate. What do you think will happen to the rate at which drops fall from the faucet if you rub a soapy finger around the end of the faucet? Try it! Were you right?

2.3   WATER DROPS ON WAXED PAPER

To do this experiment you will need:
- eyedropper
- water
- waxed paper

Use an eyedropper to place a small drop of water on a flat sheet of waxed paper. (Be sure to use an eye-dropper that has been thoroughly rinsed with water to remove any soap.) Look carefully at the drop from the side. What do you see that makes you believe water sticks together? What do you see that indicates water is not attracted to wax?

As you have observed, the forces that hold water to-gether compete well with the force of gravity that tends to flatten the drop into a thin film. You can increase the weight of the water drops by making them bigger. Make a number of globs of water of increasing size on the waxed paper. Put two drops in one glob, three drops in another, four in another, and so on. Place the drop and the globs in a row so you can compare them. What happens to the glob's shape as you in-crease its weight by adding more drops?

2.4 PREDICTIONS ABOUT SOAPY WATER ON WAXED PAPER

To do this experiment you will need:
- eyedropper
- soapy water
- water
- waxed paper

In Experiment 2.2, you saw how soap changes water's stickiness. Now see if you can use that information to make a prediction. Predict how the shape of soapy water drops and globs on waxed paper will compare with the water drops and globs you made in the last experiment.

If you do not have the drops and globs of water from the last experiment, make them again on waxed paper. Then test your prediction by putting drops and globs of soapy water on the same sheet of waxed paper. Look at the soapy water drops and globs from the side. Compare them with the drops and globs of water. Was your prediction correct? If it wasn't, you may be able to use what you have seen here to rethink your prediction.

2.5 TUG OF WAR

To do this experiment you will need:
- adult to help you
- fine black pepper
- rubbing alcohol
- bubble-making solution
- flat white plate
- plastic container (the kind frozen whipped topping comes in will work well)
- water
- eyedroppers
- soap
- sink
- food coloring

Moving Pepper Across Water

Fill a plastic container halfway with water. After the water stops moving, sprinkle a small amount of finely ground black pepper evenly over the surface of the water. **Ask an adult** to help you hold an eyedropper that contains rubbing alcohol close to the water's surface. (Be sure to handle the rubbing alcohol carefully, as it is both toxic and flammable. When you are finished with the experiment, **ask an adult** where to dispose of the liquid properly.) Carefully squeeze one drop of alcohol onto the center of the pepper-covered water surface, as shown in Figure 5. Which way does the pepper move? As the alcohol dissolves, the pepper will begin to return. What happens when you add another drop of alcohol to the same place?

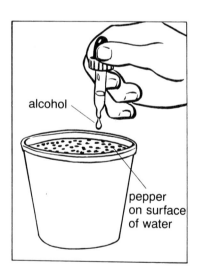

alcohol

pepper on surface of water

5) Sprinkle pepper on the surface of some water. Then, add a drop of alcohol to the center of the peppered surface. What happens?

Thoroughly clean the container before you repeat the experiment. This time, place the drop of alcohol near one side of the peppered water surface. What happens when the drop is added at this location?

Thoroughly clean the container and eyedropper. Then repeat the experiment using a drop of liquid (soap) from a bubble-making solution instead of alcohol. What happens when a drop of the soap solution is added to the center of the pepper?

Surface Force

Why does the pepper move away from the alcohol or soap? One possible explanation is that the drop hits the water and pushes the pepper away. Another explanation is that the water surface pulls itself together more strongly than the surfaces of alcohol or soap solutions. The forces holding alcohol or soap solutions together are weaker than those holding water together. As a result, water wins the "tug of war." It pulls itself together, dragging with it the surfaces of the weaker alcohol or soap that it surrounds.

To test the first explanation, see whether a drop of water will push the pepper away. But first, thoroughly clean the materials and sprinkle a new layer of pepper on some water. Then let a drop of water fall on the pepper-coated surface. Does the drop push the pepper away? Which of the two explanations in the last paragraph seems to best explain what you observed?

Now you can test the explanation that water's surface is stronger than the surfaces of alcohol or soapy water. Place a drop of food coloring on a clean, flat, white plate. Add a few drops of water and spread the colored water out into a thin layer. Next, dip your finger in alcohol and touch it to the center of the thin film of colored water. What happens? How can you explain what you observe? How is this experiment similar to the one you did with a peppered water surface?

Thoroughly clean the plate. Then repeat the experiment. But this time, dip your finger into a bubble-making solution instead of alcohol. Can you predict what will happen? Were you right?

2.6   ANOTHER TUG OF WAR

To do this experiment you will need:
- light cotton thread
- plastic drinking straw
- dishwashing detergent
- plastic container (the kind frozen whipped topping comes in will work well)
- water
- bubble-making solution
- sink
- glass tumbler

Make a loop from a piece of light cotton thread. Place the irregular-shaped loop of thread on the surface of some water in a plastic container as shown in Figure 6a. Dip the tip of a plastic straw into some bubble-making solution to wet it with soap. Then place the tip of the straw within the loop of thread (see Figure 6b). What happens to the thread? How can you explain what happens?

Make another loop from a piece of light cotton thread. Then close the drain in a kitchen sink. Add some water and dishwashing detergent to make a sudsy layer. Dip the open end of a glass tumbler into the sudsy layer. A soap film will form across the glass. Wet the loop of thread in the soapy water and carefully place it on the soap film in the glass. Touch the soap film inside the loop with a dry finger. What happens to the loop of thread? Why do you think it happens?

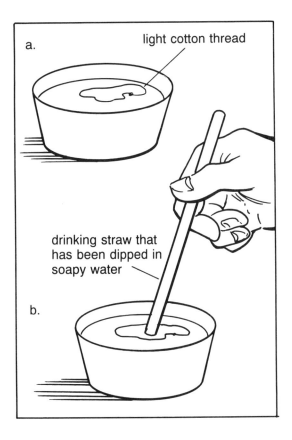

a.

light cotton thread

drinking straw that has been dipped in soapy water

b.

6a) Place a loop of light cotton thread on the surface of some water.

b) Dip the tip of a drinking straw into some bubble-making solution. When all the liquid has drained away, touch the tip of the straw to the water *inside* the loop of thread. What happens?

2.7   A DELAYED TUG OF WAR

To do this experiment you will need:

- water
- bubble-making solution
- plastic container (the kind frozen whipped topping comes in will work well)
- small plastic cup
- cooking oil
- eyedroppers or plastic drinking straws

Place some water in a small plastic cup. Use an eyedropper or a drinking straw to add some cooking oil to the water. Does the oil dissolve in the water? Does the oil sink or float in water?

Nearly fill a clean plastic container with cold water. After the water stops moving, use an eyedropper or a drinking straw to place a single glob (5 or 6 drops) of cooking oil on the center of the water surface. Then, using another clean eyedropper or drinking straw, place a single drop of bubble-making solution on the center of the oil layer. It will take a little time for the soap to work its way down through the oil to the water. That's why this is called a delayed tug of war. While you wait, you may enjoy watching the colored bands that form on the oil layer. What happens when the soap finally reaches the water? Can you explain why it happens?

Science Principle: Surface Tension

You have seen that water holds together very well. So well, in fact, that it appears to have a skin—a skin strong enough to support a steel paper clip or needle. It is the same skinlike surface that supports the weight of insects such as water striders, which walk on the surface of water. The strength with which a surface holds itself together can be measured with a balance like the one shown in Figure 7.

A film of liquid adheres (sticks) to the circle of wire attached to the left side of the balance. Weights are added to the pan on the right side of the balance. This

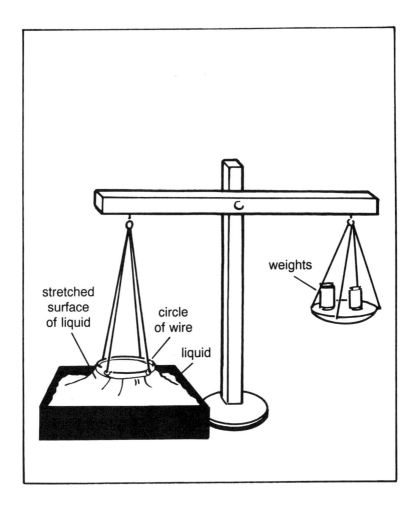

weights

stretched surface of liquid

circle of wire

liquid

7) Measuring the surface tension of a liquid.

lifts and stretches the surface of liquid attached to the wire. Finally, the liquid is stretched until it pulls apart. The force needed to stretch the liquid surface to its breaking point is measured by the weight added to the right side of the balance. This force divided by the length of the surface film that is being stretched is called the *surface tension* of the liquid. Since tension is a force that causes a material to stretch, you can see why this measurement is called *surface tension.*

The surface tensions of some common liquids are given in Table 1. As you can see, water's surface is considerably stronger than either alcohol or a soap solution. Surface tensions were measured in dynes per centimeter of the surface film's length. A dyne is a force equal to the weight of one gram.

TABLE 1
THE SURFACE TENSION OF SOME COMMON LIQUIDS

Liquid	Temperature °C	Surface Tension (dyne/cm)
Grain alcohol	20	26.8
Glycerine	20	63.1
Mercury	20	465.0
Olive oil	20	32.0
Soap solution	20	25.0
Water	0	75.6
Water	20	72.8
Water	60	66.2

Based on the information in Table 1, what happens to the strength of water's skin as its temperature increases? Which liquid in the table has a stronger skin than water? Which of the liquids in the table has the weakest skin?

2.8   A BUBBLE AND A FLAME

To do this experiment you will need:
- adult to help you
- small plastic funnel
- shallow container
- bubble-making solution
- matches
- candle and candleholder

Pour some bubble-making solution into a shallow container. Rub the rim and inside of a small funnel with the soapy solution. Then dip the wide end of the funnel into the solution. A soap film will form across the funnel opening. Notice how the film moves toward the narrow part of the funnel. A soap film always shrinks to form a surface that has the least possible area.

Ask an adult to light a candle in a candleholder. Dip the wide end of the funnel into the bubble-making solution to form a film across the funnel opening. Blow a bubble on the end of the funnel. *Ask the adult* to hold the stem of the funnel close to the base of the candle flame as shown in Figure 8. What happens to the flame?

PUZZLER 2.1
Why do you think the flame was extinguished when the funnel with its attached bubble was held near it? Compare your explanation with the one on page 95.

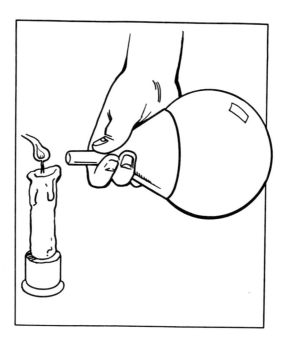

8) What happens when the stem of a funnel on which a bubble has been blown is held near the base of a candle flame?

2.9   MEASURING THE STRENGTH OF A LIQUID'S SKIN

To do this experiment you will need:

- adult to help you
- stiff cardboard
- pencil
- paper clips
- small paper cup
- straight pin
- modeling clay
- water
- rubbing alcohol
- plastic square 5 centimeters (2 inches) on a side
- 12-inch ruler
- shears
- small, sharp nail
- thread
- pliers
- matches
- shallow container
- bubble-making solution
- identical pair of tall, slender cans

You can measure the skin strength of different liquids by doing an experiment similar to the one described in the science principle on page 26. A simple balance can be made by tracing the outline of a 12-inch ruler on a sheet of stiff cardboard. Use shears to cut out the cardboard rectangle or **ask an adult** to cut it out with a sharp knife. Make dots at the positions shown in Figure 9a. Then use a small, sharp nail to make holes through the cardboard at these points.

Use the nail to support the balance beam at its midpoint, as shown in Figure 9b. Support the ends of the nail with a pair of identical tall cans. Place an unfolded paper clip in each of the holes at the ends of the beam. From the paper clip on the right hand side of the beam, use thread to suspend a small paper cup. Use a small nail to make holes in the cup that will allow you to attach thread, as shown.

From the left end of the balance, suspend a square plastic plate that is 5 centimeters (2 inches) on a side. You can cut the square from a plastic cover such as the kind found on coffee cans or margarine tubs. **Ask an adult** to use pliers to push a straight pin through the center of the square. If this is difficult, the adult can heat the end of the pin in a match flame. The adult can then use the pliers to bend the end of the pin (see Figure 9c).

If the beam is not balanced (level), add a small piece of modeling clay to the light side (the side that is tilted up). Move the modeling clay along the beam until it balances.

Place the plastic square on some water in a shallow

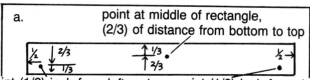

a. point at middle of rectangle, (2/3) of distance from bottom to top

½   2/3   1/3   ½
    1/3   2/3

point (1/2) inch from left end of rectangle, (1/3) of distance from bottom to top

point (1/2) inch from right end of rectangle, (1/3) of distance from bottom to top

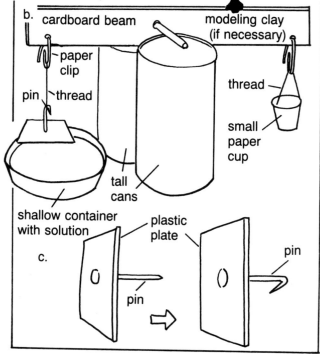

b. cardboard beam
modeling clay (if necessary)
paper clip
pin   thread
thread
small paper cup
tall cans
shallow container with solution
plastic plate
pin
c.
pin

9) A balance can be used to measure the strength of a liquid's skin.

a) The beam.

b) The assembled balance.

c) Making the plate: Cut out a square piece of plastic 5 centimeters (2 inches) on a side. To hang the plate from the balance beam, **ask an adult** to use pliers to push a straight pin through the center of the plate. Use the same pliers to bend the sharp end of the pin. Connect the plate to the paper clip at the end of the beam with a loop of thread.

container. To measure the strength of the liquid's skin, gently add small paper clips to the paper cup on the right side of the balance. How many paper clips does it take to break the water's skin?

Repeat the experiment with soapy water in the container. How many paper clips are required to break the skin on soapy water? How many paper clips are required if you use alcohol?

Science Principle: The Molecules in Water's Skin

Water's skin is very strong. Its strength is indicated by its high surface tension, which is the result of the strong forces that attract one water molecule to another. Each water molecule (H_2O) contains two hydrogen atoms (H) and one oxygen atom (O) (see Figure 10a). Like molecules of all substances, water molecules have no net electric charge. They are neutral because they have an equal number of positive and negative charges. The charges in a water molecule, however, are not evenly spread. One end of the molecule, where the two hydrogen atoms predominate, is slightly positive; the other end of the molecule is slightly negative. As a result, water molecules are said to be polar. Because they are polar, water molecules attract one another electrically (see Figure 10b). The negative end of one molecule is attracted to the positive end of another.

To see one effect of water's polar molecules, charge a plastic ruler by rubbing it with a cloth. Then bring the ruler slowly toward a thin stream of water flowing from a faucet. You will see the water stream bend toward the charged ruler.

In the middle of a glass of water, the water molecules are attracted equally in all directions (see Figure 11a). This is not true of molecules on the surface of the liquid. There, molecules are attracted only inward and

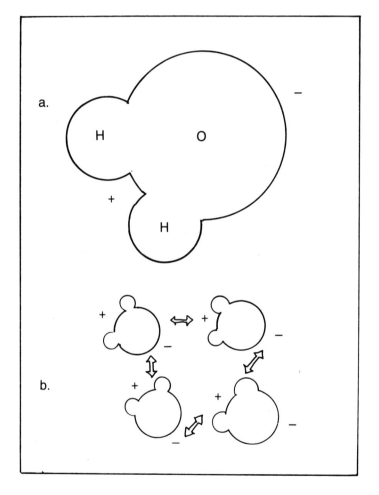

10a) A diagram of a water molecule.

b) Because water molecules are polar, they attract one another.

sideways by other water molecules beneath and beside them (see Figure 11b). The pulls to the side cancel one another—a molecule is pulled to the right as strongly as it is to the left. But there is nothing to counteract the strong inward pull. This inward pull on the surface molecules holds them tightly together. It is this

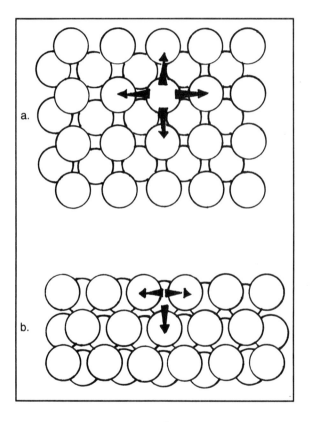

11a) Water molecules within the liquid are pulled equally in all directions.

b) Water molecules on the surface of the liquid are pulled inward. The sideways forces cancel. (There is as much pull to the right as there is to the left.)

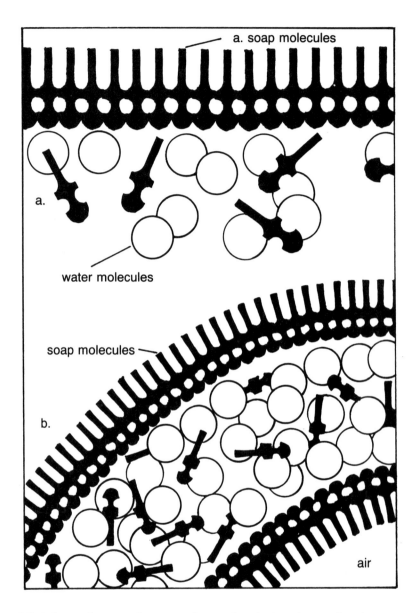

a. soap molecules

a.

water molecules

soap molecules

b.

air

12a) Soap forms a layer on the surface of water and gets between water molecules beneath the surface.

b) In a bubble, soap molecules form a layer on both the inner and outer sides of the bubble film. In between these layers, there is a mixture of soap and water molecules.

force that causes water to act as if it has a skin. And it is this inward force that explains water's high surface tension—its resistance to being pulled apart.

Soap molecules get between water molecules. One end of a long soap molecule is attracted to water; the other end is not. The result is a layer of soap molecules on the surface (see Figure 12a). The increased distance between the water molecules reduces the attractive forces. The molecules in a soap solution are held together with enough strength to form a stretchable film, but not so strongly that they pull together into drops the way water bubbles do.

When a bubble is blown in soapy water, the soap

PUZZLER 2.2
Dip a camel's-hair brush in a glass of water. Notice that the bristles remain spread out. Now remove the brush from the water. Notice that the bristles now stick together. Can you explain why the bristles stick together out of water but not in water?

PUZZLER 2.3
In Experiment 1.2, you found that bubbles blown in water quickly collapse. Adding several drops of soap solution to the water enabled you to blow bubbles that persisted. After all the experiments you have done in this chapter, why do you think water bubbles collapse while longer-lasting bubbles can be made by adding soap to water?

molecules form a layer on the surface of the bubbles (see Figure 12b). This soapy surface reduces evaporation and makes the bubble last longer.

PUZZLER 2.4

Add cold water to a sink so that the entire bottom of the sink is covered. Use scissors to cut a flat, boat-shaped piece from a sheet of aluminum foil. Hold the flat boat while a friend spreads a thin layer of bubble-making solution or dishwashing liquid to the wide stern (rear end) of the boat. Then carefully place the boat on the water with its stern near one side of the sink. Why does the boat move forward, apparently driven by its soapy "motor"?

PUZZLER 2.5

Gently place a plastic berry box on the surface of some water in a sink. As you can see, the basket rests on the water surface but dents its skin just as a paper clip does. Add a small piece of waxed paper to the basket and it still floats. But now carefully remove the waxed paper and replace it with a piece of paper towel. Why does the "boat" sink when its cargo is changed?

The San Francisco Exploratorium has some wonderful giant bubble experiments that you will want to see if you visit that city. The exploratorium makes its bubble solution by mixing 2/3 cup of Dawn™ and Joy™ dishwashing detergent with 1 tablespoon of glycerine and 1 gallon of distilled water. Can you prepare a better bubble-making mixture?

The Life and Size of Bubbles

Anyone who has been in a supermarket knows that there are many brands of soap and dishwashing liquids. You might wonder: Is one brand of dishwashing liquid better than another for making bubbles?

In this chapter, you will carry out tests to find out whether larger and longer-lasting bubbles are associated with a particular brand of dishwashing liquid. You will also investigate various additives, such as glycerine and sugar, to see whether they enhance the art and science of making bubbles. And, you will test a number of recipes (including your own) for making bubbles, as you search for the world's best bubble-making solution.

3.1 BIG BUBBLE HEMISPHERES

To do this experiment you will need:
- bubble-making solution
- measuring cup
- yardstick
- paper or notebook
- vinegar
- bubble wands you can buy in a store
- several brands of dishwashing liquid (try to include Dawn™ and Joy™)
- soft water
- plastic drinking straw
- pencil
- paper towels
- smooth surface, such as the top of a kitchen counter
- covered containers to hold bubble-making solutions

Prepare a bubble-making solution from each one of the several brands of dishwashing liquid. To do this, add 1 tablespoon of the dishwashing liquid to 1 cup of soft water. This makes a solution that is 1 part dishwashing liquid and 16 parts water. Pour the mixture into a container and stir it gently with a drinking straw to avoid making suds.

Take the first solution you prepared and pour some onto a smooth counter. Use your hand to spread the liquid over an area about 50 centimeters (20 inches) across. Dip a drinking straw into the solution. Lift the straw straight up from the solution and let any excess drain from the straw. Place the end of the straw and the solution that remains in it at the center of the wet area on the counter. Blow into the liquid that remains at the end of the straw. Continue to blow until the bubble breaks. You will be amazed at the size of the bubble hemisphere you can make.

Maximizing Bubble Size

When the bubble breaks, it will leave a circle of droplets along its outside edge, or circumference (see Figure 13). Use a yardstick to measure the diameter of the circle (the length across its middle). What was the diameter of the bubble you blew with this solution?

Record this number on a piece of paper or in a notebook. Repeat the experiment several times to be sure the results are always about the same. Do you know the average diameter of the bubbles?

13) When a bubble breaks, it leaves a ring of tiny droplets along its circumference.

41

To determine the average, add all of the diameters you wrote down, and divide that number by the number of times you recorded the diameter. If you blew five bubbles and their measurements were 9, 6, 4, 6, and 5, you would calculate the average in the following manner: 9 + 6 + 4 + 6 + 5 = 30 ÷ 5 (the number of bubbles you recorded) = 6. The average (or mean) diameter of those bubbles would be 6. What is the average diameter of the bubbles you have blown?

Wipe off the counter with a paper towel that has been moistened with vinegar. Repeat the experiment using each of the solutions you have made as well as the bubble-making solution you bought. With which solution can you blow the largest bubble?

Many recipes for bubble-making solutions suggest that the solution be left for a day or two before being used to make bubbles. After 24 to 48 hours, repeat this experiment. Does the additional time seem to make any difference in the size of the bubbles you can make?

3.2 THE LIFE SPAN OF BUBBLES

To do this experiment you will need:
- paper or notebook
- pencil
- vinegar
- plastic cover about 12-15 centimeters (5-6 inches) in diameter (the kind found on a frozen whipped topping container will work well)
- tape
- paper towels
- plastic drinking straw
- other similar covers with smaller and larger diameters
- stopwatch or watch with a second hand

Place a plastic cover upside down on a counter. Pour one of the solutions you used in Experiment 3.1 onto the cover. Pour enough of the solution to completely coat the cover's surface. Place a drinking straw in the center of the liquid and blow a bubble with the same diameter as the cover. Remove the straw and begin timing. If air currents are a problem, you can tape several sheets of paper together to build a protective cylinder around the bubble. Record the length of time the bubble lasts.

Repeat the experiment several times to be sure the results are about the same each time. Record the times on a piece of paper or in a notebook and find the average lifetime of a bubble of this solution. Wipe off the cover with a paper towel that has been moistened with vinegar.

Repeat the experiment for each of the bubble-making solutions you prepared, as well as the one you bought. Which solution provides bubbles with the longest average life span?

Use the liquid with the longest life span to find out whether the diameter of a bubble affects its life span. You can do this by using covers that are larger and smaller than the one you used before. Do big bubbles last longer than little bubbles?

Does the age of a bubble-making solution (the time since it was made) have any effect on the life span of the bubbles made with the solution?

3.3 DILUTED BUBBLES AND BUBBLE SIZE

To do this experiment you will need:
- water
- plastic drinking straw
- yardstick
- paper or notebook
- covered containers to hold bubble-making solutions
- dishwashing liquid from which you made the biggest bubbles in Experiment 3.1
- measuring cup
- paper towels
- pencil
- vinegar
- smooth surface such as the top of a kitchen counter

Diluting Bubble-making Solutions

For this experiment, use the dishwashing liquid from Experiment 3.1 that gave you the biggest bubbles. Start with the pure dishwashing liquid. Pour about 1/4 cup of it into a container. Next, prepare a bubble solution that is diluted 1:8 (1 to 8). To make such a dilution, use the measuring cup to measure out 1 ounce of the pure dishwashing liquid. Pour this liquid into a second container. Add 7 ounces of water to the measuring cup and pour it into the second container also. You have now diluted the original volume of liquid from 1 to 8 ounces by adding 7 ounces of water (see Figure 14a). The dishwashing liquid was spread through a volume of 1 ounce. It is now spread through 8 ounces so it is 1/8 as concentrated as it was before. We say it has been diluted 1:8.

Rinse the measuring cup thoroughly. Then measure out 1 ounce of the solution you just made and pour it

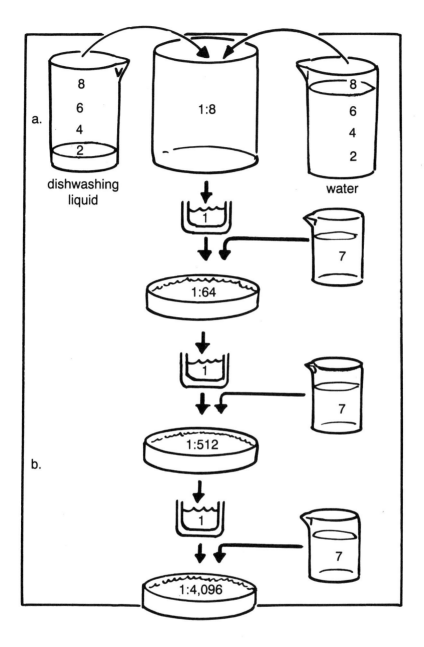

14a) If you add 7 ounces of water to 1 ounce of dishwashing liquid, you have diluted the liquid 1:8.

b) Successive dilutions give 1:64, 1:512, and 1:4,096.

into a third container. As before, dilute this liquid 1:8 by adding 7 ounces of water (see Figure 14b). The concentration of this solution is now 1/64 as concentrated as the original dishwashing liquid. After all, 1/8 x 1/8 = 1/64.

If you now dilute this solution 1:8 , as shown in Figure 14b, you will have a solution that is 1/512 as concentrated as the original solution. Diluting this solution 1:8 will make it about 1/4,096 as concentrated as the original solution. You will then have five different bubble-making solutions with concentrations of 1, 1:8, 1:64, 1:512, and 1:4,096. Save these solutions. You will use them in Experiments 3.3 and 3.4.

Measuring Bubble Diameter

To find out whether diluting the dishwashing liquid affects the size of the bubble hemispheres you can blow, begin by pouring some of the pure dishwashing liquid onto a smooth counter. Use your hand to spread the liquid over an area about 50 centimeters (20 inches) across. Dip a drinking straw into the solution. Lift the straw straight up from the solution and let any excess drain from the straw. Place the end of the straw and the solution that remains in it at the center of the wet area on the counter. Blow into the liquid that remains at the end of the straw. Continue to blow until the bubble breaks.

Use a yardstick to measure the diameter of the circle of droplets left by the bubble. What was the diameter of the bubble you blew with this solution?

Record this number on a piece of paper or in a

notebook. Repeat the experiment several times to be sure the results are always about the same. What is the average diameter of the bubbles you can blow using this solution?

Wipe away the bubble-making solution on the counter with a paper towel that has been moistened with vinegar. Repeat the experiment using the second solution (the original dishwashing liquid diluted 1:8).

Do the same for each of the other diluted liquids. Does diluting the liquid affect the size of the bubble hemispheres you can blow? If so, how does dilution affect bubble size?

3.4   DILUTION AND BUBBLE LIFE SPAN

To do this experiment you will need:
- sheets of paper
- paper or notebook
- paper towels
- dishwashing liquid and diluted solutions you made in Experiment 3.3
- plastic cover about 12–15 centimeters (5–6 inches) in diameter (the kind found on a frozen whipped topping container will work well)
- tape
- pencil
- vinegar
- stopwatch or watch with a second hand
- plastic drinking straw

Place a plastic cover upside down on a counter. Pour the first of the solutions (the pure dishwashing liquid) you used in Experiment 3.3 onto the cover. Pour enough to completely cover the surface. Place a drinking straw in the center of the liquid and blow a bubble with the same diameter as the cover. Remove the straw and begin timing. If air currents are a problem, you can tape several sheets of paper together to build a protective cylinder around the bubble. Record the length of time the bubble lasts.

Repeat the experiment several times to be sure the results are about the same each time. Record the bubbles' life spans on a piece of paper or in a notebook. What is the average life span of a bubble of this liquid? Wipe off the counter with a paper towel that has been moistened with vinegar.

Repeat the experiment for each of the diluted solutions you prepared for Experiment 3.3. Does diluting the dishwashing liquid affect the average life span of the bubbles? If it does, for which dilution do the bubbles last the longest?

Science Principle: Hygroscopic Substances

Some substances, such as calcium chloride, are said to be *hygroscopic*. Such substances attract moisture. Bags of calcium chloride are often hung in damp places to remove humidity (water vapor) from the air. Because glycerine is hygroscopic and dissolves in water, many recipes for bubble-making solutions include glycerine. Glycerine's attraction for water is believed to reduce the evaporation of soap-bubble films and thus improve the life span of bubbles. In the next experiments, you will test the effect of glycerine on bubble life span and size.

3.5 THE EFFECT OF GLYCERINE ON BUBBLE LIFE SPAN

To do this experiment you will need:
- measuring cup
- eyedropper
- dishwashing liquid from which you made the biggest bubbles in Experiment 3.1
- plastic cover about 12–15 centimeters (5–6 inches) in diameter (the kind found on a frozen whipped topping container will work well)
- soft water
- plastic drinking straw
- covered containers to hold eight different bubble-making solutions
- glycerine **(Caution: don't touch glycerine, you might be allergic to it. Don't mix it with anything other than water or soapy water.)**

Prepare a bubble-making solution using the best bubble-making dishwashing liquid from Experiment 3.1. Slowly pour 1/2 cup of the dishwashing liquid into 1.9 liters (2 quarts) of soft water. Stir the solution with a drinking straw, being careful not to make suds. Pour 1 cup of this bubble-making solution into each of 8 small containers.

Place the containers on pieces of paper labeled 1, 2, 3, 4, 5, 6, 7, and 8. Use an eyedropper to add 10 drops of glycerine to the container labeled 1. Add 20 drops of glycerine to container 2, 30 drops to container 3, and so on until you have added 70 drops to container 7. Add nothing to the solution in container 8. When you are finished with this experiment, be sure to save these solutions to use in Experiment 3.6.

Place a plastic cover upside down on a counter. Pour some of the first solution (the one with 10 drops of glycerine) onto the cover. Pour enough to just cover the surface. Place a drinking straw in the center of the thin liquid layer and blow a bubble with the same diameter (length across its middle) as the cover. Remove the straw and begin timing. If air currents are a problem, you can tape several sheets of paper together to build a protective cylinder around the bubble. Record the length of time the bubble lasts.

Repeat the experiment several times to be sure the results are about the same each time. Record the bubble's average life span on a piece of paper or in a notebook. Wipe off the cover with a paper towel that has been moistened with vinegar.

Repeat the experiment for each of the other 7 solutions. Does glycerine affect the average life span of the bubbles? If it does, how many drops per cup provide bubbles with the longest life span?

3.6   THE EFFECT OF GLYCERINE ON BUBBLE SIZE

To do this experiment you will need:
- plastic drinking straws
- pencil
- smooth surface, such as the top of a kitchen counter
- yardstick
- paper or notebook
- covered containers to hold bubble-making solutions
- the 8 solutions prepared in Experiment 3.5 **(Caution: don't touch glycerine, you might be allergic to it. Don't mix glycerine with anything other than water or soapy water.)**

Does glycerine affect bubble size? To find out, you can use the 8 different bubble-making solutions you prepared in Experiment 3.5. Pour some of solution 1 onto a smooth counter. Use a straw to spread the liquid over an area about 50 centimeters (20 inches) across. Dip another straw into the container that holds the solution. Lift the straw straight up from the solution and let any excess drain from the straw. Place the end of the straw and the solution that remains in it at the center of the wet area on the counter. Blow into the liquid that remains at the end of the straw. Continue to blow until the bubble breaks. You can measure the diameter of the bubble, as you did in Experiment 3.1.

What was the diameter of the bubble you blew with this solution? Record this number on a piece of paper or in a notebook. Repeat the experiment several times to be sure the results are always about the same. What is the average diameter of the bubbles you can blow using this solution?

Wipe off the counter top with a paper towel that has been moistened with vinegar.

Repeat the experiment using each of the solutions from Experiment 3.5. Does the amount of glycerine affect bubble size? Can you be sure of obtaining larger bubbles by increasing the amount of glycerine in the bubble-making solution?

3.7 THE EFFECT OF OTHER SUBSTANCES ON BUBBLE LIFE SPAN

To do this experiment you will need:
- plastic drinking straw
- pencil
- sheets of paper
- sugar
- Jell-O™ (powder)
- stopwatch or watch with a second hand
- dishwashing liquid from which you made the biggest bubbles in Experiment 3.1
- plastic cover about 12-15 centimeters (5-6 inches) in diameter (the kind found on a frozen whipped topping container will work well)
- yardstick
- paper or notebook
- tape
- Karo™ corn syrup
- Certo™ (powder)
- Kool-Aid™ (powder)
- covered containers to hold bubble-making solutions
- smooth surface such as the top of a kitchen counter

Some recipes for bubble-making solutions substitute sugar or other substances for glycerine. Try some of these substitutes to see whether they increase the life span or size of bubbles. You can start with the same solution you used in Experiment 3.1. Divide it into smaller equal volumes, and add different amounts of such things as sugar, Karo™, Jell-O™, Certo™, Kool-Aid™, etc. Do any of these substances have an effect on bubble life span or size?

3.8 HUMIDITY, TEMPERATURE, AND BUBBLES

How does humidity affect the life span and size of bubbles? Design an experiment of your own to find out.

How does temperature affect the life span and size of bubbles? Design and carry out an experiment of your own to find out. Can bubbles be frozen? If they can, do they last longer than bubbles at room temperature?

The record life span for a bubble was set by Eiffel Plasterer who was also known as Professor Bubbles. Plasterer was able to keep a bubble for 340 days! He blew the bubble on a small dish inside a big, wet wide-mouth jar. He sealed the jar with a screw-on cap and kept it in his basement workshop. The bubble never broke; it simply shrank until it disappeared.

Perhaps you will set a new record for keeping bubbles. But don't be upset if you are not successful on your first try; the professor had been making and studying bubbles for more than sixty years.

3.9 RECIPES FOR BUBBLE-MAKING LIQUIDS

To do this experiment you will need:
- soft water
- plastic drinking straw
- pencil
- sheets of paper
- covered containers to hold bubble-making solutions
- stopwatch or watch with a second hand
- plastic cover about 12-15 centimeters (5-6 inches) in diameter (the kind found on a frozen whipped topping container will work well)
- sugar
- yardstick
- paper or notebook
- tape
- smooth surface such as the top of a kitchen counter,
- liquid dishwashing detergents, including Joy™ and Dawn™
- glycerine **(Caution: don't touch glycerine, you might be allergic to it. Don't mix it with anything other than water or soapy water.)**

There are a variety of recipes for bubble-making so-lutions that you can find in various books. Commercial bubble-making solutions that you can buy in stores do not list the ingredients. Can you guess why they don't?

Listed below are some of the recipes you can find in other books. You might like to try some, or all, of these recipes and see which one allows you to make the biggest and longest-lasting bubbles. You might also like to try some recipes of your own. Perhaps you will come up with the world's best bubble-making solution.

Recipes for bubble-making solutions:

- Dissolve 1/2 cup of liquid dishwashing detergent in 1 cup of soft water.

- Dissolve 2 tablespoons of liquid dishwashing detergent, a pinch of sugar, and a tablespoon of glycerine in 1 cup of soft water.

- Dissolve 1/4 cup of liquid dishwashing detergent and 12 drops of glycerine in .95 liter (1 quart) of soft water.

- Dissolve 30 milliliters (1 ounce) of liquid dishwashing detergent and 50 drops of glycerine in 2 cups of soft water.

- Dissolve 1/3 cup of Dawn™ liquid dishwashing detergent and 1/2 tablespoon of glycerine in 1.9 liters (2 quarts) of soft water.

- Dissolve 30 milliliters (1 ounce) of Joy™ liquid dishwash-ing detergent in .95 liter (1 quart) of soft water.

- Dissolve 1 tablespoon of Blue Dawn™ liquid dishwashing detergent in 1 cup of warm soft water.

- Dissolve 2 tablespoons of liquid dishwashing detergent (Joy™ or Ajax™) in 1 cup of warm soft water.

- Dissolve 4 tablespoons of soap powder in .95 liter (1 quart) of warm soft water. Allow the solution to stand for three days. Stir in 1 tablespoon of sugar.

- Don't forget to make up your own personal recipe for a bubble-making solution!

A bubble, as you know, is very fragile. When something dry, even something as small as a speck of dust, touches its thin skin, it makes a hole in the bubble's surface.

Bubbles in Motion

You have looked closely at bubbles on a wand, table, or countertop and you have seen how they change with time. But it's also fun to watch bubbles as they fall, move sideways, and even rise into the air. In this chapter, you will concentrate on moving bubbles. You will investigate the effect of bubble size and thickness on the rate at which bubbles fall. You will see how the speed at which a bubble falls is affected when the bubbles are filled with gases other than air, such as carbon dioxide and helium. You will find a way to make bubbles float on a layer of gas, and you will learn how to change or control a bubble's flight path by using moving air and electricity.

4.1 FALLING AIR-FILLED BUBBLES OF DIFFERENT SIZE AND THICKNESS

To do this experiment you will need:
- bubble wand
- bubble pipe
- bubble-making solution and container to hold it

Make some bubbles by swinging a bubble wand through the air. Watch the bubbles as they fall. Can you tell whether big bubbles fall faster or slower than little ones?

When you swing a soap film-covered wand through the air, you can make a variety of bubbles. Some are big; some are little; some have a thin wall; some have a thick wall. It may not be easy to tell whether the size of a bubble affects its rate of fall by watching a random bunch of bubbles. However, it is easy to see that a bubble falls more slowly than a tennis ball or a baseball, even if it is bigger than a soccer ball. In fact, bubbles fall at a steady speed. A baseball or a tennis ball accelerates (moves faster and faster) as it falls.

Timing Bubbles

Use the bubble pipe you made in Experiment 1.2 to make bubbles of different sizes. First, blow a large bubble. Twist the pipe to free the bubble, and let it fall. Then find out how long it takes the bubble to fall from eye level to the floor. If you do not have a stopwatch or a watch with a second hand, you can count, "1, 2, 3, 4, 5," as fast as you can while the bubble is falling. You will find that it takes just about 1 second to count to 5 very fast. If you count to 5 three times while the bubble falls to the floor, it took about 3 seconds for the bubble to fall.

Repeat the experiment several times to be sure the results are about the same. Next, repeat the experiment using smaller bubbles. How long does it take the smaller bubbles to fall the same distance? Does the size of a bubble affect the rate at which it falls?

Bubble Thickness and the Rate of Fall

To see how the thickness of a bubble affects its rate of fall you will need to have patience. You know that sometimes after you blow a bubble, a film is still stretched across the wand or pipe. Since much of the soap film was carried away in the previous bubble, the next bubble will generally contain less soap. So, the second bubble will have a thinner wall than the first one.

Blow some bubbles. After you release each bubble, look quickly to see if a film remains. If it does, quickly blow a bubble about the size of the previous one. If possible, watch the two bubbles as they fall. Try to judge, as best you can, which bubble falls faster. If you cannot produce the second bubble fast enough to watch both of them fall, then time their falls through the same distance separately. Try the experiment several times. Does the thickness of a bubble affect its rate of fall?

Science Principle: Air Resistance and Area

A baseball and a tennis ball will fall side by side in air. In a vacuum, where there is no air, a bubble and a baseball will fall side by side as well. When an object falls in air, the gas pushes upward against the object. This push is called *air resistance*. It keeps the object from falling as fast as it would in a vacuum. For bubbles, air resistance becomes equal to the bubble's weight soon after it begins to fall. When that happens, the bubble falls at a steady speed called its *terminal velocity*. Baseballs and skydivers reach terminal velocities as well, but it takes longer. A bubble reaches its terminal velocity almost immediately.

To see how the area (the amount of surface) of an object affects air resistance, try the following experiment. Take two sheets of paper. Fold one sheet as many times as you can. Leave the other sheet flat. Drop both pieces of paper at the same time. Which one falls faster? How does the amount of area (surface) affect the air resistance of a falling object?

The same is true with bubbles. Big bubbles fall more slowly than small ones of the same weight. The big bubble has more surface for the air to push against.

PUZZLER 4.1
How would you find the terminal velocity of a bubble?

4.2 "FALLING" HELIUM-FILLED BUBBLES

To do this experiment you will need:

- round 9-inch balloon
- spool
- modeling clay
- bubble wand
- helium-filled balloon (**Caution: do not breathe in helium—it can be dangerous.**)
- twistie
- plastic drinking straw
- bubble-making solution
- bicycle tire pump
- stopwatch or watch with a second hand

Buy a helium-filled latex balloon. You can find them at many florist or greeting card stores. Bring a twistie with you. Ask the person who fills the balloon to tie off the neck of the balloon with the twistie. Do not let them tie a knot in the neck of the balloon.

Once you reach home, attach the balloon to one end of a spool (see Figure 15a). Place a straw in the hole at the other end of the spool. Use modeling clay to seal the straw to the spool.

Use your fingers to seal off the balloon as you carefully remove the twistie from the balloon's neck. Dip the tip of the straw into some bubble-making solution. Have a friend dip a wand into the same liquid. Gently touch the tip of the straw to the center of the soap film on the wand and carefully release some gas from the balloon to form a helium-filled bubble at the end of the wand (see Figure 15b). Release the bubble by twisting the wand as you have done before. What happens to the bubble?

Dip the end of the straw into the bubble-making

solution and release a little gas from the balloon to make some helium-filled bubbles. If you make the bubbles very small, they will fall instead of rising in the air the way big helium-filled bubbles do. How big do the bubbles have to be before they will rise?

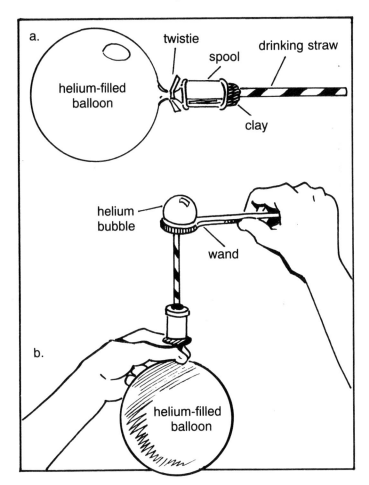

15a) Attach a helium-filled balloon to a drinking straw through a spool.

b) Dip the tip of the straw into a bubble-making solution. Touch the straw to the soap film on a wand and use helium to blow a bubble on the wand.

4.3   "FALLING" CARBON DIOXIDE-FILLED BUBBLES

To do this experiment you will need:

- water
- round 9-inch balloon
- spool
- modeling clay
- bubble wand
- small, clear flask or bottle
- seltzer tablets
- twistie
- plastic drinking straw
- bubble-making solution
- bicycle tire pump
- stopwatch or watch with a second hand

You can compare the rates of fall (terminal velocities) of air-filled and carbon dioxide-filled bubbles. But first, you will need some carbon dioxide. You can make relatively pure carbon dioxide by dropping seltzer tablets into water. The bubbles that form are carbon dioxide gas.

Collecting Carbon Dioxide

To make and collect carbon dioxide, pour about 25 milliliters (1 ounce) of water in a small, clear flask (like the one shown in Figure 16a) or into a small bottle (like an aspirin bottle that holds 250 tablets). Break two seltzer tablets into small pieces and drop them into the neck of a round 9-inch balloon (see Figure 16b). Pull the

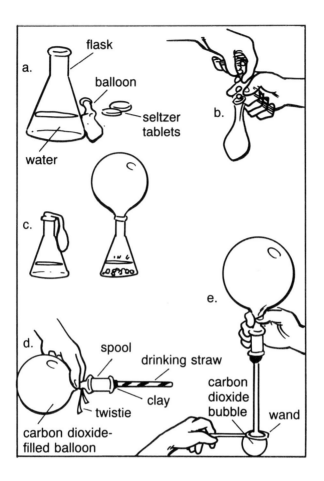

16a) Pour about 25 milliliters (1 ounce) of water into a clear flask or bottle.

b) Break two seltzer tablets into small pieces. Drop them into a balloon.

c) Attach the balloon to the neck of the flask or bottle and lift the balloon so the tablets fall into the water and generate carbon dioxide.

d) Attach the carbon dioxide-filled balloon to a drinking straw through a spool.

e) Use balloon, straw, and wand to produce a carbon dioxide bubble.

neck of the balloon over the top of the bottle or flask, as shown in Figure 16c. Raise the balloon so that the pieces of seltzer fall into the water. Watch the reaction between the seltzer tablets and water. You will see bubbles of carbon dioxide released from the water. The gas will fill the bottle and then the balloon. Gently swirl the flask or bottle to release as many carbon dioxide bubbles as possible from the water. When the bubbles stop forming, carefully remove the gas-filled balloon from the flask or bottle. Seal off the neck of the balloon with a twistie.

Attach the balloon to one end of a spool (see Figure 16d), as you did with the helium-filled balloon. Place a straw in the hole at the other end of the spool. Use modeling clay to seal the straw to the spool.

Use your fingers to seal off the balloon as you carefully remove the twistie from the balloon's neck. Dip the tip of the straw into some bubble-making solution. Have a friend dip a wand into the same liquid. Gently touch the tip of the straw to the center of the soap film on the wand and carefully release some gas from the balloon to form a carbon dioxide-filled bubble at the end of the wand (see Figure 16e). Release the bubble from a height about equal to the position of your eye. Measure the time it takes the bubble to reach the floor. You can use a stopwatch, a watch with a second hand, or you can count "1, 2, 3, 4, 5," as described in Experiment 4.1.

Timing Carbon Dioxide-filled Bubbles
Blow and time the fall of as many carbon dioxide-filled

bubbles as you can, using the balloon, straw, and wand. Does the thickness of a bubble affect its rate of fall? Does the size of a bubble affect its rate of fall? Find the average time it takes for a carbon dioxide-filled bubble to reach the floor.

Repeat the experiment with air-filled bubbles of about the same size. You can fill the balloon with air using a bicycle tire pump. How do the falling speeds (terminal velocities) of carbon dioxide-filled bubbles and air-filled bubbles compare?

Repeat the experiment once more using a balloon that has been filled with air from your lungs. How do the terminal velocities of lung air-filled bubbles compare with carbon dioxide-filled bubbles and air-filled bubbles?

PUZZLER 4.2
Why do carbon dioxide-filled bubbles fall faster (have a larger terminal velocity) than air-filled bubbles? Since we breathe out carbon dioxide, why don't bubbles filled with lung air fall as fast as carbon dioxide-filled bubbles?

4.4   CARBON DIOXIDE AND FLOATING BUBBLES

To do this experiment you will need:
- 4-liter (1-gallon) plastic pail
- water
- seltzer tablets
- bubble wand
- bubble-making solution

Since carbon dioxide is heavier than an equal volume of air, you might expect that an air-filled bubble would float in an atmosphere of carbon dioxide. After all, helium-filled bubbles float in air. To test this idea, you will need to make a carbon dioxide atmosphere.

To prepare such an atmosphere, add water to a 4-liter (1-gallon) plastic pail until the depth of the water is about 2–3 centimeters (1 inch). Drop about a dozen seltzer tablets into the water. As you know, the fizzing reaction between the seltzer and water produces carbon dioxide.

To see if air-filled bubbles will float on the carbon dioxide, blow some bubbles with a wand. Let the bubbles fall into the pail. You may have to move the pail so that it lies beneath a falling bubble. Will an air-filled bubble float on a carbon dioxide atmosphere?

Do carbon dioxide-filled bubbles have longer life spans than ordinary bubbles? How can you find out?

4.5   CHANGING A BUBBLE'S "FLIGHT PATTERN"

To do this experiment you will need:
- bubble pipe
- sheet of cardboard about the size of a piece of notebook paper
- bubble-making solution

This experiment requires a little patience and a lot of practice. But once you get the hang of it, you will be glad you stayed with it. It works best in a place where there are no air currents.

Use a bubble pipe, like the one you built in Experiment

1.2, to make a good-sized bubble. As the bubble starts to fall, wave a flat sheet of cardboard above it, as shown in Figure 17. You will find that you can stop the bubble's fall. In fact, you can make the bubble rise. By waving the cardboard at the proper angle above the bubble, you can make the bubble move right and left, forward and backward, as well as up. Once you have mastered the technique, you will be able to guide the

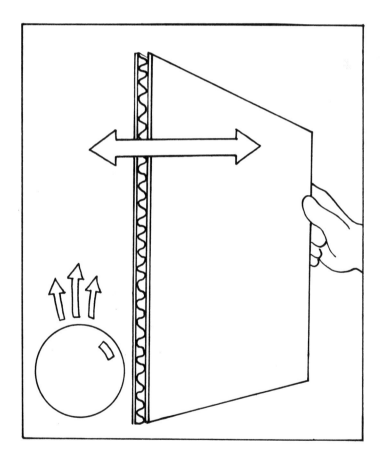

17) Waving a sheet of cardboard back and forth will allow you to control the motion of a bubble.

bubble along any path you wish. The only limit will be the bubble's life span.

Can you use the same cardboard sheet to keep a helium-filled bubble from rising? Can you keep the helium-filled bubble suspended so that it neither rises nor falls?

What is the mysterious force that allows you to guide bubbles along any path you choose? Bernoulli would know!

Science Principle: Bernoulli's Principle

Bernoulli's principle states that where the speed of a fluid (gas or liquid) is high, the pressure is low; where the speed of a fluid is low, the pressure is high. To see what this means, hold a Ping Pong ball in the mouth of an upside-down funnel, as shown in Figure 18a. Blow into the stem of the funnel and release the ball. You will find that as long as you blow, the ball will stay in the funnel (despite gravity). Because the pressure of the fast-flowing air above the ball is so much less than the pressure of the still air below the ball, the upward force on the ball is greater than its weight (see Figure 18b).

4.6   MOVING BUBBLES WITH ELECTRICITY

To do this experiment you will need:
- plastic ruler or comb
- sink with faucet
- bubble-making solution
- old phonograph record
- cloth or paper towel
- bubble wand
- plastic drinking straw

This experiment should be done on a cool, dry day

when there is very little humidity. Humidity causes an electric charge to "leak" away.

Making Electricity

Rub a plastic ruler or comb on a cloth or a paper towel. This will place a charge of one sign (+ or -) on the

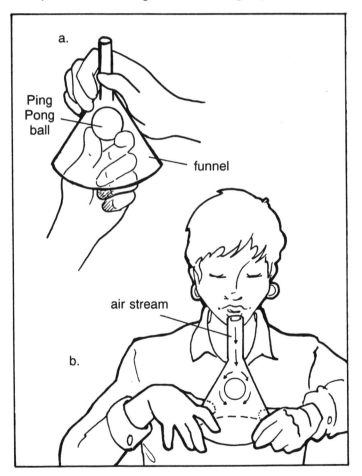

a.

Ping Pong ball

funnel

air stream

b.

18a) Hold a Ping Pong ball in the mouth of an inverted funnel.

b) If you blow into the stem of the funnel, the ball will stay in the funnel and defy gravity.

plastic and the opposite charge on the cloth or paper. Bring the charged plastic close to (but don't touch) a thin stream of water flowing from a faucet. You will see the stream bend toward the charged plastic.

Although water molecules are not charged, they are polar (see Figure 10). That is, one end of each molecule is slightly positive and the other end is slightly negative. If a negatively charged object is held near water, the positive ends of the water molecules are attracted to it. If a positively charged object is held near water, the negative ends of the molecules are pulled toward it.

Attracting Soap Bubbles

You might expect that soap bubbles, which contain water, would also be attracted to an electric charge. To see if they are, dip a bubble wand and a straw into some bubble-making solution. Then use the straw to blow a bubble on the wand. Ask a friend to hold the wand while you charge a plastic ruler or comb by rubbing it with a cloth or paper towel.

Move the charged plastic slowly toward the bubble (see Figure 19a). What happens to the bubble as the plastic approaches?

Repeat the experiment using an old phonograph record that has been rubbed with a cloth. Does the record appear to be charged? How can you tell?

Ask your friend to use a bubble wand to make some bubbles while you charge a plastic ruler or comb. What happens when you bring the charged plastic above

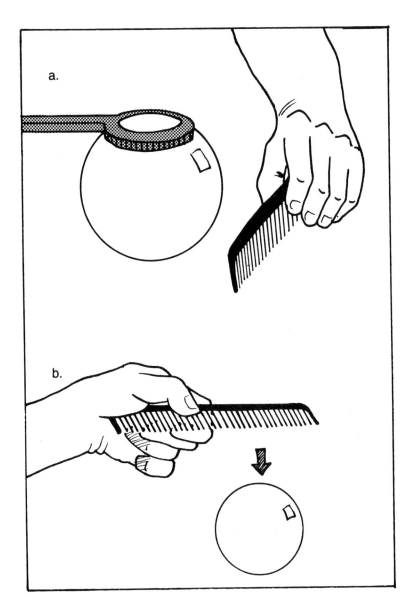

19a) Hold a charged ruler or comb near a bubble suspended from a wand. What happens to the bubble?

b) Hold a charged ruler or comb above and close to a slowly falling bubble. What happens to the bubble?

one of the falling bubbles (see Figure 19b)? Can you use the charged plastic to stop a bubble's fall? Can you use an old phonograph record that has been rubbed with a cloth to stop a bubble's fall? If not, repeat the experiment after your friend succeeds in blowing a thin bubble that falls very slowly.

Cover a smooth counter top with a thin layer of soapy water. Let a lemon-size bubble fall onto the wet surface. Can you make the bubble move by bringing a charged ruler, comb, or record close to it?

The pressure of the air trapped within a bubble is greater than the pressure of the air outside its skin. When a tiny hole appears in a bubble's skin, the air rushing out through the opening shatters the bubble's skin, producing thousands of tiny droplets.

Bubbles, Light, and Color

You have seen the beautiful and changing colors that appear in bubbles. Perhaps you have also noticed images, like those in mirrors, that can be seen when light is reflected from the surface of a soap film. In this chapter, you will look more closely at those colors and compare the images with those seen in mirrors.

5.1   DRAINING BUBBLE FILMS

To do this experiment you will need:
- string
- small glass
- long, narrow, shallow container
- plastic drinking straws
- tape
- food coloring

- bubble-making solution (try several, including one made by adding 1/3 cup Dawn™ and 1/2 tablespoon (about 150 drops) of glycerine to 2 quarts of soft water)

- bubble wand (such as the kind that comes with bubble-making solutions, or one you make from a cotton pipe cleaner wound in a circle and attached to a heavy wire)

Dip a bubble wand into a bubble-making solution. Hold the wand in front of your face, as shown in Figure 20a. Stand with a window at your back and a dark background in front of you. Turn the wand slowly until you see light reflected from the surface of the soap film across the wand. Watch carefully as the soap film drains. You will see bands of color move slowly down the wand. Eventually, when the film becomes very thin, a dark band will form across the top of the film. The film in this dark area is less than 0.00001 centimeters (4 millionths of an inch) thick.

Giant Bubble Colors

To see the colors in a draining soap film in more spectacular fashion, build a frame like the one you made in Experiment 1.3 to produce giant bubbles. But this time, run a 90-centimeter (3-foot) and a 60-centimeter (2-foot) length of string through one of the two drinking straws. Tie the ends of the 60-centimeter (2-foot) length string together to make a handle from which the frame can be suspended (see Figure 20b). Run the 90-centimeter (3-foot) long piece of string through a second straw. Tie its ends together and pull the string until the knot lies within one of the straws.

Pour enough bubble-making solution into a long,

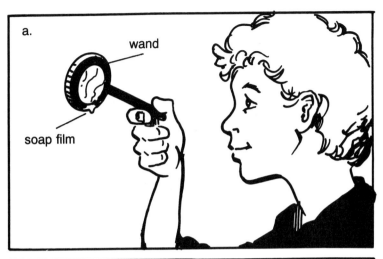

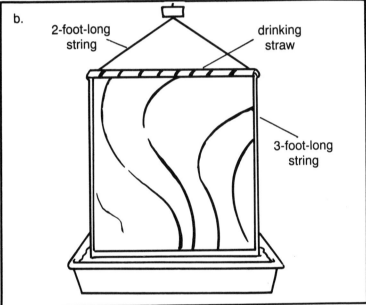

20a) A soap film drains on a bubble wand.

b) A large soap film drains on a frame made from drinking straws and string.

narrow, shallow container to fill it to a depth of about 2–3 centimeters (1 inch). The straw-and-string frame (see Figure 20b) can now be lowered by its string handle into the bubble-making solution in the shallow container. Be sure both straws and all the string are submerged in the solution. Use the string handle to lift the frame upward and watch the soap film drain. Again, be sure there is a dark background behind the soap film. Then look at light coming from behind you as it reflects from the film.

To free yourself so that you can obtain the best viewing angle, attach the string handle to the bottom of a cupboard, the back of a box or chair, or something similar. You should be able to see wide bands of various color. What happens to the colored bands as the film drains? What happens to their widths? To the distance between them? How many different colors can you see?

After the film has drained awhile, you will see a dark region forming at the top of the film. This is the very thin layer of film you saw before. If you think there is nothing in that dark area, try touching it with your finger. What happens?

Bubbles From Colored Liquids

If you make bubbles from a colored liquid, will the bubbles have the same color as the liquid? To find out, pour some bubble-making solution into a small glass. Add a few drops of food coloring and stir gently with a straw. Dip the end of a straw and a wand into the colored liquid. Place the wet end of the straw on the film across the wand and blow a bubble on the wand. Is the bubble the same color as the liquid? What colors can you see in the bubble? Do you see colors other than the color of the liquid?

If you think there is no food coloring in the bubble, try this. Blow a bubble using the colored liquid. Let the bubble fall on a damp, smooth counter top. Break the bubble by touching it with your finger. Look closely at the ring of tiny droplets left by the broken bubble. What evidence do you have that there was food coloring in the bubble?

Save the materials you used in this experiment. You will use them again in Experiment 5.2.

5.2   SOAP FILMS, IMAGES, AND PLANE (FLAT) MIRRORS

To do this experiment you will need:
- plane (flat) mirror, such as a hand mirror **(Caution: if you drop a glass mirror and break it, do not pick up the glass. Ask an adult to help you.)**
- materials used in Experiment 5.1

Use the drinking straw-and-string frame and the bubble-making solution you used in Experiment 5.1 to make a large soap film. This time concentrate on the images you see reflected from the film. Are the images right side up or inverted (upside down)?

Compare the images seen in the soap film with those you can see in a plane mirror, such as a hand mirror, held near the film. How do the sizes of the images seen in the film compare with those seen in the mirror? What is similar about the images seen in the mirror and film? What is different about them?

Two Images

If you look closely, you will see that there are two images in an ordinary glass mirror. Place your fingertip on the surface of such a mirror. You will see a faint image in front of a brighter image. Light reflected from the front surface of the glass produces the faint image. Light reflected from the silvered surface on the back of the glass forms the brighter image.

A soap film has a front and a rear surface too. However, the film is so thin that the images are very close together.

Make another large soap film with your straw-and-string frame. After the film has drained for a while, a dark region will appear near the top of the film where it has become very thin. You will not be able to see images in this part of the film. Can you see through this portion of the film?

SURPRISE 5.1
It probably surprised you to find that you could see images in one part of a soap film and not in the other. Why should you be able to see images in a thick soap film but not in a very thin one? After you have thought about it, compare your explanation with the one on page 97.

5.3   PREDICTING A BUBBLE'S BURST

To do this experiment you will need:

- bubble-making solution
- plastic drinking straw
- paper or notebook
- 1/3 cup Dawn™ dishwashing liquid and 1/2 tablespoon (about 150 drops) glycerine in 2 quarts of soft water **(Caution: don't touch glycerine, you might be allergic to it. Don't mix glycerine with anything other than water or soapy water.)**
- tape
- sheets of paper
- pencil
- stopwatch or watch with a second hand
- plastic cover about 12-15 centimeters (5-6 inches) in diameter (the kind found on a frozen whipped topping container will work well)

Place a plastic cover upside down on a counter. Pour some of the bubble-making solution onto the cover—enough to completely cover the surface. Place a drinking straw in the center of the solution and blow a bubble with the same diameter as the cover. If air currents are a problem, you can tape several sheets of paper together to build a protective cylinder around the bubble.

Watch a few large bubble hemispheres and time their life spans with a stopwatch or a watch or clock with a second hand. See if you can figure out a way to predict, within a few seconds, when a bubble is going to burst.

5.4 BUBBLES, IMAGES, AND CURVED MIRRORS

To do this experiment you will need:
- mirror
- old newspapers
- bubble pipe
- concave mirror, such as shaving or makeup mirror
- wide, shallow container to hold the bubble-making solution
- bubble-making solution
- well-lighted window or door
- bubble wand
- convex mirror, such as right-hand side-view mirror on a car or truck

Look into a mirror. There you will find your image. Light, such as sunlight or light from lamps, is reflected from your face. When this light reaches the mirror, it is reflected again. Some of the reflected light enters your eye. The reflected light that enters your eye allows you to see yourself in the mirror. (For a more detailed look at how images are formed, read *Experiments with Light and Mirrors*, another *Getting Started in Science* book.)

Seeing Yourself in a Mirror

You have seen your image in a mirror. You may also have seen your image reflected from a smooth pond or puddle. If you look closely, you can see your image in a soap bubble, too. In fact, you can see two images!

Make a bubble pipe, such as the one you used in Experiment 1.2. Pour some bubble-making solution into a wide shallow container. Dip the open end of your bubble pipe's bowl into the solution. Stand on newspapers (to avoid having bubbles fall on the floor) in front of a well-lighted window or door and blow a large bubble.

Twist the bowl of the pipe to set the bubble free and then catch the bubble on the pipe. Look into the bubble. Can you see images? How many images of yourself can you see? (The images of you are probably quite dark because the light reflected by the bubble is coming from behind you.)

Convex and Concave Mirrors

Notice that the images reflected from the front surface of the bubble are right side up. They are reflected from a *convex* surface (see Figure 21). A convex surface is one that bulges outward like the front of an eyeball.

The rear surface of the bubble is a *concave* surface — one that curves inward like a saucer. What do

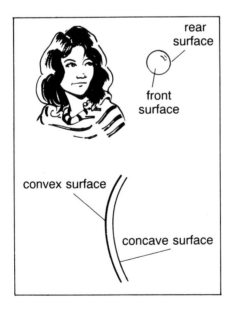

21) As you look into a bubble, the front surface is convex. The rear surface is concave. How do the images reflected from these two surfaces compare?

you notice about images reflected from the rear (concave) surface of the bubble? Are they right side up or inverted (upside down)?

Are the images seen on the front (convex) surface of the bubble larger or smaller than the original objects? How about the images on the rear (concave) surface of the bubble?

Repeat the experiment several times until you can see the images clearly. Take time to enjoy the color changes in the images as the soap film drains.

Images on Curved Surfaces

Now do the same experiment, using one of the plastic wands that come with the bottles of bubble-making solutions you can buy in a store. The bubble you capture this time will probably be smaller than the one you made with a bubble pipe. Are the images smaller too? Are both images smaller? Are the images on the front surface of the bubble inverted? Are the images on the rear surface inverted?

The images you see in an ordinary (*plane*) mirror are reflected by a flat surface. As a result, these images (such as the image of your own face) are the same size as the original objects. The images you saw in a bubble were reflected from curved surfaces—the surfaces of a sphere. To compare the images you see in bubbles with those seen in curved mirrors, you will need a concave and a convex mirror. These curved mirrors are shown in Figure 22.

A shaving or makeup mirror has a concave surface.

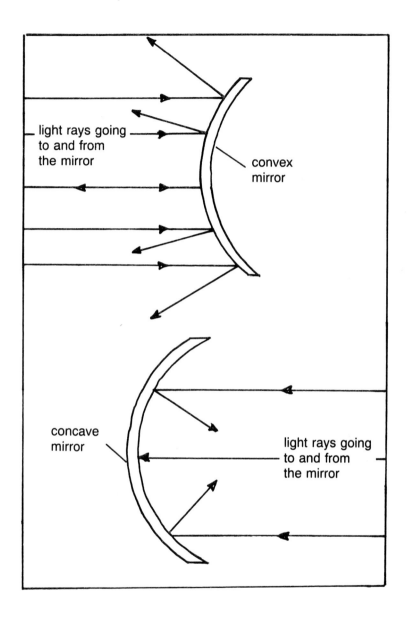

light rays going to and from the mirror

convex mirror

concave mirror

light rays going to and from the mirror

22) Both a convex and a concave mirror can be used to reflect light and form images. Arrows pointing toward the mirror indicate light rays coming to the mirrors. Arrows pointing away from the mirror show light rays reflected from the mirrors.

Hold such a mirror close to your face. Is the image larger or smaller than your actual face? Is this like the image you saw on the concave (rear) surface of the bubbles?

Now move farther from the mirror. Watch your image carefully as you move. You will reach a point where the image is inverted just as it was on the concave surface of the bubble. How is it different than the image you saw in the bubble? Move still farther away from the mirror. How does the image change? How does the size of the image compare with the size of the object when the object is far from the mirror? Is this image similar to the ones you saw reflected from the concave surface of the bubble?

Now look into a convex mirror. If you cannot find a convex mirror, you can use a pair of sunglasses. The front surfaces of the sunglasses are convex (they curve outward). Place the glasses or the mirror on a table in a well-lighted room. Look into the front surface of the mirror or one lens of the sunglasses. Notice that you can see your image and the images of a number of nearby objects. How do these images compare with the ones you saw in the front surface of the bubble?

PUZZLER 5.1
What will you expect the images to look like if you hold a concave mirror so that it reflects light coming from distant objects located outside a window?

Under the watchful eye of an adult, and through a pair of safety glasses, look at the bubbles that form when a beaker of water is heated. At first, the bubbles, which are filled with water vapor, collapse as they rise to the surface. But when the water reaches the boiling temperature, the bubbles burst only when they reach the surface. It is these bubbles that carry gaseous water from the liquid into the air.

Bubble Geometry

In the bubble experiments you have done in earlier chapters, you have focused on single, round (spherical) bubbles, and on soap films that were flat before being filled with air or other gases. But bubbles, such as those found in a dishpan or a bathtub, usually come in clusters and they are not always spherical. Soap films, too, can be more complex. In this chapter, you will look at soap films formed in specially built "cages" and at multiple bubbles—double bubbles, bubble chains, and various bubble clusters. The experiments you do will give you some insight into the geometry of bubbles.

6.1 CAGED SOAP FILMS

To do this experiment you will need:
- adult to help you
- white cotton pipe cleaners
- plastic drinking straw
- wide, deep container to hold bubble-making solution
- cutting pliers
- bubble-making solution
- large, shallow plastic dish

So far, you have looked at round (spherical) bubbles made from flat soap films. What shape would a bubble have if it was made with a wand shaped like a cube, pyramid, or prism?

3-D Bubble Wands

To find out, you can build these three-dimensional wands from white cotton pipe cleaners (see Figure 23a). You will be glad you did because you will see some bubble film shapes you would not expect.

Use pieces of pipe cleaner that are about 8 centimeters (3 inches) long. Join the pieces by using pliers to bend and squeeze the end of one piece over the end of another. You can make as many shapes as you like, but try to make a cube, a prism, and a pyramid (see Figure 23b). Attach a pipe cleaner handle to each shape so you can easily dip the structures into the bubble-making solution.

Bubble Cubes, Pyramids, and Prisms

Try to avoid making suds by gently dipping the prism into the bubble-making solution. You will find that surface tension pulls the soap film into a shape that looks

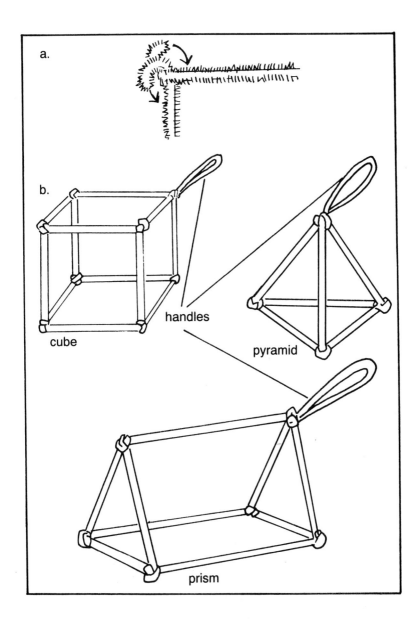

a.

b.

handles

cube

pyramid

prism

23a) Pipe cleaners can be cut and joined by using pliers. Squeeze the end of one cleaner over the end of another to make firm connections

b) Use pipe cleaners to build an open cube, prism, and pyramid.

like the one in Figure 24a. Look at the film. Look very closely. How many films meet along a line? How many lines meet at a point? How many films meet at a point?

Wet the end of a straw by dipping it into the bubble-making solution. Place the wet end of the straw at the center of the films. Gently blow a very small bubble there. What is the shape of the bubble? How does its shape compare with the shape of the frame? If you blow through the cube as you might through a wand, what is the shape of the bubbles that fly off the cube?

Repeat the experiment with the pyramid. This time, the film will look like the one in Figure 24b. Again, look closely at the film and answer the same questions about films, lines, and points. What is the shape of the bubble you get when you use a straw to gently blow a bubble at the center of the films?

If you blow through the pyramid as you would through a wand, what is the shape of the bubbles that fly from the pyramid?

Repeat the experiment with the prism. This time, the film will look like the one in Figure 24c. Again, look closely at the film and answer the same questions about films, lines, and points. What is the shape of the bubble you get when you use a straw to gently blow a bubble at the center of the films?

If you blow through the prism as you would through a wand, what is the shape of the bubbles that fly from the prism?

Other Shapes
Build frames with other shapes and test them in the

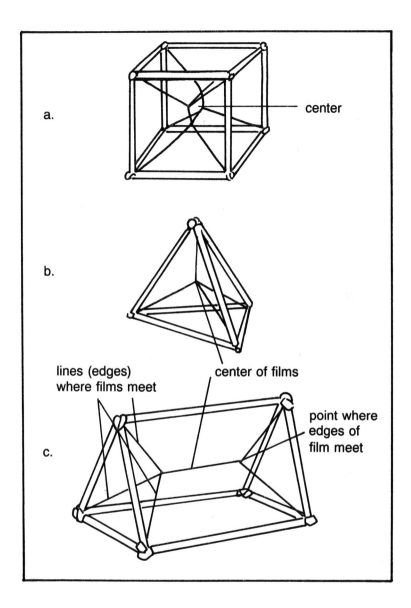

a. — center

b.

lines (edges)
where films meet

center of films

point where
edges of
film meet

c.

24) Films take on a regular, predictable shape when they
    form inside open frames.

a) A soap film in an open cube.

b) A soap film in an open pyramid.

c) A soap film in a triangular prism.

same way. How many films meet along a line? How many lines meet at a point? How many films meet at a point? If you blow through these frames as you would through a wand, what is the shape of the bubbles that fly away?

Pour some bubble-making solution into a large, shallow plastic dish. Wet the entire inside surface of the dish with the liquid. Then blow into the bubble-making solution through a straw. Make a large mass of bubbles and observe them carefully. For any intersection of bubbles you choose to look at, how many films meet along a line? How many lines meet at a point? How many films meet at a point?

SURPRISE 6.1
You were probably surprised to find that when soap films, such as bubbles, come together they do so in a very regular manner. What regularities did you find about the way soap films join?

6.2   DOUBLE BUBBLES AND SHRINKING BUBBLES

To do this experiment you will need:
- bubble wand
- bubble-making solution
- plastic drinking straw

Dip a small bubble wand and a straw into a bubble-making solution. Use the straw to blow a bubble on the bottom of the wand. Remove the straw. Then push it back through the bubble film to the center of the bubble. (What would happen if you tried to push a dry straw through the bubble?)

Can you blow a second bubble inside the first one? You will find it easier to blow a bubble inside another one if you continue to blow into the straw as you pull it out of the first bubble. Once you succeed, see how many small bubbles you can blow inside one big bubble.

Use the straw to blow a bubble on the wand. Remove the straw, touch it to the bottom surface of the bubble (not inside the bubble), and blow a second bubble. Now insert the straw through the surface of the first bubble. Slowly, suck air from the bubble. What happens to the size of the bubble? Can you reduce the double bubble to a single bubble? Can you do the same thing if you insert the straw into the second bubble?

6.3 BUBBLE CHAINS AND CLUSTERS

To do this experiment you will need:
- bubble wand
- bubble-making solution
- plastic drinking straw

Dip a small bubble wand and a straw into a bubble-making solution. Use the straw to blow a small bubble on the bottom of the wand. Remove the straw from the bubble. Then touch the end of the straw to the bottom surface of the bubble and blow a second bubble. Remove the straw and blow a third bubble on the bottom of the second. See how many bubbles you can make in your bubble chain. You may find it easier to do if you have a friend hold the wand while you make the bubble chain.

Use the wand and straw to make a two-bubble chain. Both bubbles should be very nearly the same size. You will find it helpful to have a friend hold a second wand under the bubbles. This will help to hold the bubbles in place while you use the straw to blow a

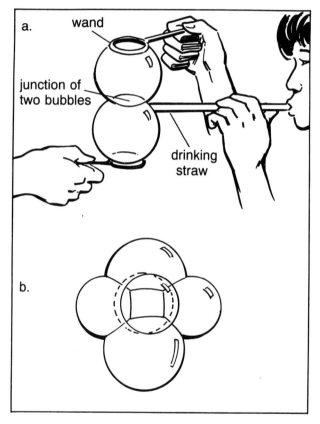

25a) A double bubble between two wands. Start the first of four more bubbles on the junction between the two bubbles.

b) A six-bubble cluster. What will be the shape of a seventh bubble blown at the center of the cluster?

bubble on the circle where the two bubbles meet (see Figure 25a). Make the bubble big enough to cover 1/4 of the circle's circumference. Then blow three more bubbles, each 1/4 the circumference of the circle to make a six-bubble cluster (see Figure 25b). Finally, place the straw in the very center of the cluster and blow one more bubble. What is the shape of this seventh bubble?

Repeat the experiment, but this time blow six bubbles along the circle where the two bubbles meet. Blow a final bubble in the center of this cluster. What is the shape of this ninth bubble?

Repeat the experiment again, but this time blow eight bubbles along the junction of the original two-bubble chain. Predict the shape of the final (eleventh) bubble that you blow at the center of the cluster.

Design your own bubble clusters. Can you predict the shape of the bubble you will get when you blow one at the center of each of your clusters?

Answers to Puzzlers and Surprises

Puzzler 1.1

A bubble's film contains water and soap. When a bubble strikes a dry surface, the liquid in the film is absorbed by the dry material and the bubble collapses. When a bubble lands on a wet surface, it absorbs as much liquid as it loses. Consequently, it maintains itself. Look at a bubble that has landed safely on a woolen blanket. It is supported at the ends of a few tiny fibers. Very little liquid is absorbed by these few fibers. As a result, the bubble can sustain itself.

Puzzler 2.1

The forces of surface tension in the bubble's soap film pull the film together. This makes the bubble shrink. The shrinking bubble squeezes the air together, pushing it out the neck of the funnel and into the flame. If you watch the bubble closely, you will see it grow smaller with time.

Puzzler 2.2

Inside the water, the wet bristles are surrounded on all sides by water. Consequently, they are pulled equally in all directions and so remain separated. When removed from the glass, water lies only between the wet bristles not around them. Since water pulls together, the wet bristles are attracted inward toward the water and toward one another.

Puzzler 2.3

Water attracts itself so strongly that the film around bubbles blown in water pulls together to form drops. Soap gets between water molecules, reducing the attractive forces between them. The surface tension in a soap film is strong enough to hold together, but not so strong that it pulls together and forms drops.

Puzzler 2.4

The soapy water at the boat's stern does not pull on the boat as strongly as does the water at the bow. As a result, the boat is pulled forward.

Puzzler 2.5

The water's surface tension is strong enough to support the basket without breaking. Water wets a paper towel, that is, water is absorbed by the paper. Consequently, when the paper towel is added, water flows into the paper (bringing the basket below the surface) and it sinks. Waxed paper is not wet by water. As a result, the waxed paper does not pull water across the surface and the basket continues to float.

Puzzler 4.1

You could stretch a string at a known distance above the floor. At the moment the bottom of a bubble crosses the line, you would stop the watch. Dividing the distance the bubble fell by the time recorded on the stopwatch would give the bubble's terminal velocity. If a bubble falls 5.0 feet in 6.0 seconds, its terminal velocity is:

5.0 feet ÷ 6.0 seconds = 0.83 feet per second

Surprise 4.1

Helium weighs less than an equal volume of air. Therefore, it floats on air just as wood floats on water. (Wood weighs less than an equal volume of water.) If the bubble is very small, the weight of the soap film makes the overall weight of the bubble (soap film + helium) greater than an equal volume of air and so the bubble sinks.

Puzzler 4.2

Carbon dioxide weighs more than an equal volume of air. Consequently, it will require more air resistance (a greater speed) before it reaches its terminal velocity. Only a small percentage of exhaled air is carbon dioxide; it is mostly nitrogen and oxygen.

Surprise 5.1

To explain why we see no image (and therefore no reflected light) from a very thin soap film, we assume that light is made up of waves consisting of crests (peaks) and troughs (dips) (see Figure 26a). These waves, which are very short or 0.00004 to 0.00007 centimeters (0.000016 to 0.000028 inches), are reflected from both the front and rear surface of the soap film. The portion of a wave reflected from the front surface of the film is inverted (see Figure 26b). That is, a crest is reflected as a trough and vice-versa. A wave reflected from the rear surface, where the wave passes from liquid to air, is not inverted. A crest is reflected as a crest and a trough as a trough (see Figure 26c).

In a very thin film, waves are reflected from both surfaces at almost the same time. As a result, a crest reflected as a trough from the front surface lies almost exactly beside a crest reflected as a crest from the rear surface. The crest and trough very nearly cancel one another—the upward wave motion and the downward wave motion add to give a wave with no motion (see Figure 26d). This is similar to what happens when a crest-like pulse moving one way on a rope meets a trough-like pulse moving the other way (see Figure 26d).

As the film becomes thicker, the wave reflected from the rear surface falls farther behind the wave reflected from the front surface. When film is 1/4 wavelength in thickness, the two waves reinforce one another and we see a bright band of light. At a thickness of 1/2 wavelength, the waves again cancel and we see a dark band. Similarly, at film thicknesses of 1 wavelength, 1 1/2 wavelengths, 2 wavelengths . . . we see dark bands where the waves cancel. At thicknesses of 3/4 wavelength, 1 1/4 wavelengths, 1 3/4 wavelengths . . . the reflected waves reinforce (back up) one another and we see bright bands.

Different colors of light have different wavelengths. Therefore, the film thickness at which waves of blue light reinforce or cancel is not the same as that at which green, yellow, or red light waves cancel or reinforce.

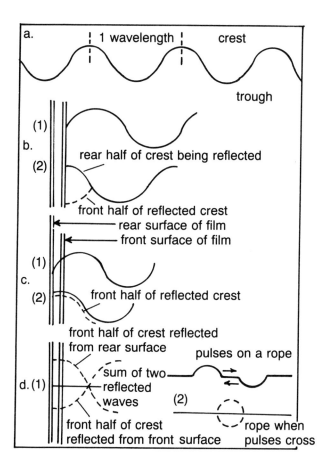

a. 1 wavelength ¦ crest

trough

(1)
b.
(2) rear half of crest being reflected

front half of reflected crest
rear surface of film
front surface of film

(1)
c.
(2) front half of reflected crest

front half of crest reflected
from rear surface
pulses on a rope

sum of two
d. (1) reflected
waves (2)

front half of crest
reflected from front surface
rope when pulses cross

26a) Light can be thought of as waves with very short wavelengths.

  b) When a light wave reflects from the front surface on a soap film (1), it is inverted (2). The second drawing (2) shows the wave after the first half of the crest being reflected has been inverted. It is reflected as a trough.

  c) When a light wave reflects from the rear surface of a soap film (1), it is not inverted (2)—a crest is reflected as a crest.

  d) In a very thin film, the waves reflected from the front and rear films cancel (1) because a crest and trough add to zero. This is similar to the way a crest and a trough cancel on a rope (2).

99

That is why you saw colored bands of light at different positions along the draining film. The thickness of the film determines which wavelengths (colors) reinforce and which cancel. Between the very thin film and 1/4-inch-thick film, none of the wavelengths completely cancel and so the film appears white.

Puzzler 5.1

Because the objects are far from the mirror, you will see inverted images that are much smaller than the objects themselves.

Surprise 6.1

From your observations, you can see that three films meet along a line. You may have noticed, too, that the angles between the films are always equal (120°). When the edges (lines) of different films meet at a point, you see four lines join. The angles between these lines are also equal (a little more than 109°). At the point where four lines meet, you find six films meeting at the same point. Other arrangements may exist for short periods of time, but they are unstable and the films quickly change until they meet as described above.

Blowing through any of the frames produces round (spherical) bubbles. Once the soap film is free of its attachments to frames, it pulls together as closely as it can. A sphere offers the smallest possible surface for forces that pull matter together. That is why the planets and drops of liquids are spheres.

Further Reading

Barber, Jacqueline. *Bubble-ology*, eds. Lincoln Bergman and Kay Fairwell. Berkeley, Calif.: Lawrence Hall of Science, 1986.

Boys, C.V. *Soap Bubbles and Forces Which Mold Them.* Garden City, N.Y.: Doubleday, 1959.

Brown, Bob. *More Science for You: 112 Illustrated Experiments.* Blue Ridge Summit, Pa.: Tab Books, 1988.

_____. *Science for You: 112 Illustrated Experiments.* Blue Ridge Summit, Pa.: Tab Books, 1988.

Herbert, Don. *Mr. Wizard's Supermarket Science.* New York: Random House, 1980.

Noddy, Tom. *Tom Noddy's Bubble Magic.* Philadelphia: Running Press, 1988.

Wood, Robert W. *Physics for Kids: 49 Easy Experiments with Mechanics.* Blue Ridge Summit, Pa.: Tab Books, 1989.

Zubrowski, Bernie. *A Children's Museum Activity Book: Bubbles.* Boston: Little Brown, 1979.

Index

A air resistance, 59
averages, 42
B balance, 31
Bernoulli's Principle, 68
breaking bubbles, 15
bubble
  chemistry, 17–38
  colored liquids, 76–77
  colors, 74–76
  cubes and other
    shapes, 89–91
  detergent, 39
  diameters, 41–42
  flame, 29
  frozen, 53
  geometry, 86–94
  hemispheres, 40
  light and color, 73–85
  making, 8
  motion, 56–72
  rate of fall, 58
  recipes, 39, 53–55
  temperature, 52–53
  wands, 10, 13–14,
    87–91
  water, 16
bursting bubbles, 79–80
C carbon dioxide bubbles,
  62–66
  life span, 66
  making, 62–64
  timing the fall, 64–65

chains and clusters, 92–94
convex and concave
  surfaces, 81–82
D delayed tug of war, 26
diluted bubbles, 44–48
diluting bubble-making
  solutions, 44–46
  effect on bubble life
    span, 47–48
  effect on maximum
    size, 46
diluting glycerine, 49
  effect on bubble life
    span, 49–50
  effect on maximum
    bubble size,
    50–51
double bubbles, 91–92
draining soap films, 73–76
E electricity, 68–72
  attraction to soap
    bubbles, 70
  bubbles, 68–72
  making, 69
  water stream, 70
exploratorium, 39
F falling carbon dioxide
  bubbles, 62–66
  effect of size, 65
  effect of thickness, 65
falling helium bubbles,
  60–61

falling lung-air-filled
balloons, 65
falling soap bubbles,
57–66
timing the fall, 57–58
floating bubbles, 66

G giant bubbles, 12–14
launching, 14
making, 12–14
wands for making,
13–14
glycerine, 39
effect on bubble life
span, 49–50

H heaping water, 18–19
helium-filled bubbles,
60–61
making, 60
humidity, 52–53
hygroscopic substances,
48–49

I images, 78–85
bubbles and curved
surfaces, 80–85
plane mirrors, 81

L life and size of bubbles,
39–55
life spans, 42–43, 52
effect of age, 43
effect of diameter, 43
effect of various
substances, 52

M mirrors, convex and
concave, 81–84

P pepper on water, 22–23

pipe, 10–12
Plasterer, Eiffel (Professor
Bubbles), 53
polar molecules, 33, 70
prisms and pyramids,
87–89

R recipes for bubble-
making solutions, 39,
53–55

S soap
films and images,
78–85
stickiness, 19–20
surface tension,
36–37
soap bubbles, 8–10
sugar, 39
surface tension, 23,
26–29, 33
balance, 31–33
effect of substance,
28
effect of temperature,
28
measuring, 30–33
molecules, 33–37
table, 28

T temperature, 53
terminal velocity, 59
tugs of war, 21–26

W wands, 10,
giant, 13–14
three-dimensional,
87–91

water
bubbles, 16
drops on waxed
paper, 20
heaping, 18–19
molecule, 33
polar molecules, 33,
70
skin, 19, 30–37
soapy, 21
stickiness, 18–28